Meltdown!

The NUCLEAR DISASTER IN JAPAN and OUR ENERGY FUTURE

Fred Bortz

TWENTY-FIRST CENTURY BOOKS
MINNEAPOLIS

TO MY GRANDCHILDREN, ELON, ELIANA, AND ALEX,
AND TO ALL YOUNG READERS WHOSE WORK AND
VOTES WILL SHAPE OUR ENERGY FUTURE
—F.B.

Twenty-First Century Books
A division of Lerner Publishing Group, Inc.
241 First Avenue North
Minneapolis, MN 55401 U.S.A.

Website address: www.lernerbooks.com

Main body text set in Bembo Std 12/15.
Typeface provided by Monotype Typography.

Library of Congress Cataloging-in-Publication Data

Bortz, Alfred B.
Meltdown! : the nuclear disaster in Japan and our energy
future / by Fred Bortz.
p.   cm.
Includes bibliographical references and index.
ISBN 978–0–7613–8660–5 (lib. bdg. : alk. paper)
1. Nuclear power plants—Accidents—Japan—Fukushima–ken.
2. Nuclear reactor accidents—Japan—Fukushima–ken. 3. Boiling
water reactors—Accidents—Japan—Fukushima–ken. 4. Nuclear
energy—Safety measures. 5. Tsunami damage—Japan—Fukushima–
ken. I. Title.
TK1365.J3B67 2012
363.17'990952117—dc23   2011029692

Manufactured in the United States of America
1 – DP – 12/31/11

CONTENTS

JAPAN.

MARCH 11, 2011.

2:46 P.M.

AN EARTHQUAKE STRIKES.

Arun Vemuri is not frightened when he feels his Tokyo office on the thirtieth floor of the Yebisu Garden Place Tower begin to sway. He knows that the building is one of the safest in the city. Like other Japanese buildings, it is designed to bend in an earthquake instead of breaking. So for the first minute, he is smiling at his coworkers and "having a swinging good time."

Then the swaying turns into wild shaking. Office equipment topples, and the jolting motion sweeps desks clear. Arun ducks under his desk.

After six long minutes, the shaking stops. Arun and his colleagues leave the office and head down thirty flights of stairs. No one seems anxious or fearful. "No rushing of feet or stomping of ground. No racing through or overtaking. Just a good old smiling saunter as if going down for a quick cup of coffee."

NO ORDINARY EARTHQUAKE

Similar scenes are taking place all over Tokyo *(above left)*. Though almost everyone seems calm, they know that this is no ordinary earthquake. Because the shaking lasts so long and skyscrapers are still swaying, this has to be a big one. The most worrisome question is this: Is the quake's epicenter (the place on Earth's surface directly above the underground spot where a quake begins) on land or in the ocean? An undersea quake could unleash a tsunami (a Japanese word for "harbor wave"), a powerful destructive wall of water rushing in from the sea.

Everyone scrambles for information. Most cell phone service is out, but the Internet is working. Twitter is buzzing with news of earthquake damage and a powerful tsunami rolling into the Tohoku region at the northern end of Honshu, Japan's main island.

Within hours, horrifying pictures and video are spreading around the world. Almost thirty thousand people in Japan are dead, injured, or missing, mostly from the tsunami.

The Great Tohoku Earthquake is the most powerful ever to strike Japan, and the tsunami makes it one of the worst disasters in that island nation's history. Yet in some ways, it is a familiar event for Japan, where earthquakes are common. The Japanese people know what it takes to recover from earthquakes and tsunamis.

NUCLEAR EMERGENCY!

What people do not yet know is that a much greater and more terrifying challenge lies ahead. That evening, news begins to spread about an emergency at the Fukushima Daiichi nuclear power plant about 260 kilometers (160 miles) northeast of Tokyo. The government of Fukushima Prefecture (state or province) warns people who live within 3 km (2 mi) to leave.

Japanese chief cabinet secretary Yukio Edano tries to reassure the public. "We have declared a nuclear emergency state to take every possible precaution," he declares at a news conference. "There is no radiation leak, nor will there be a leak."

He could not be more wrong. One reactor is already undergoing a meltdown, and two others will soon follow. It is the beginning of a disaster that will change life in Japan and alter the world's energy future.

Chapter 1

EARTHQUAKE!
TSUNAMI!
MELTDOWN!

Although it strikes suddenly, the Great Tohoku Earthquake has been building up for hundreds of years. Like all quakes, it happens because Earth's outer rocky layer, called the crust, is made up of many large, slow-moving pieces. These are called called plates.

The crust lies above another rocky layer called the mantle. The mantle is so hot that it is not completely solid. It flows in giant loops from Earth's core to the crust. The pattern is the same one you can see in a pot of boiling water on a stove. But the movement is much slower because the mantle is made of rock.

At the top of the mantle, different loops flow in different directions. The flowing mantle drags the crust with it. That explains the cracking and movement of the plates.

Most of the Pacific Ocean lies above the Pacific Plate. Japan sits just west of the Pacific Plate on three other plates. Those are the North American Plate to the north, the Eurasian Plate to the west, and the Philippine Plate to the south.

EARTHQUAKE!

Year after year, the Pacific Plate moves about 8 to 9 centimeters (3 to 3.5 inches) closer to Japan. That's about half as fast as your hair grows. It plows

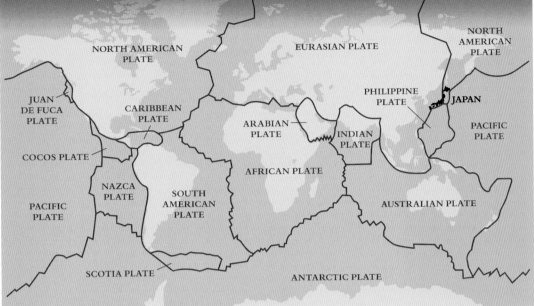

This map shows Earth's plates. Japan straddles three plates. Moving and shifting plates cause earthquakes. Millions of earthquakes have rocked Japan over the centuries, such as the Great Tohoku Earthquake in March 2011 that devastated the country.

under the North American Plate and the Philippine Plate off the east coast of Honshu, Japan's main island.

The rocks of the Pacific Plate lock with the rocks at the edges of the plates above it. That bends the upper plates downward. With every centimeter that the Pacific Plate moves, the upper plates bend more. With every centimeter, the force on the locked rocks grows. Finally, that force becomes more than the locked rocks can handle.

The rocks start to crack, crumble, and split apart. That increases the force on other nearby rocks even more. Those rocks also break apart. All along the line joining the plates, the cracking quickly spreads. That releases the bending force, and the edge of the top plate springs upward 5 to 8 meters (16 to 25 feet).

That is how the Great Tohoku Earthquake begins. Its underground starting point, called the focus, or hypocenter, is about 32 km (20 mi) beneath the epicenter on the ocean surface.

For 220 seconds, or nearly four minutes, the cracking spreads rapidly in two zones. The cracks reach a total of 300 km (185 mi) in length before they stop. Some sections of rock have shifted by as much as 60 m (200 ft).

Part of the island of Honshu is now 2.4 m (8 ft) closer to North America. The quake is so powerful that it even shifts Earth's tilt. The North Pole and the South Pole are 10 to 25 cm (4 to 10 in) from where they were before.

TSUNAMI!

The sudden upward movement of the top plate creates a huge tsunami. A bulge of water about 180 km (110 mi) wide begins traveling toward the Tohoku coast. In the deep ocean, a tsunami can travel at the speed of a jet plane. It travels slower in shallower regions.

As the tsunami reaches shallow water near the Tohoku shore, it slows and water piles up even higher. The giant wave begins surging onto the closest land, about 72 km (45 mi) west of the epicenter, about 10 to 20 minutes after the quake. An hour later, it reaches the major city of Sendai, where it begins flooding the airport.

Most Japanese coastal towns have walls to keep them safe from tsunamis. But this one is higher than the walls can handle. At some narrow inlets, it reaches as high as 39 m (128 ft). It roars ashore. It uproots trees, knocks buildings off their foundations, and carries cars and trucks in rivers of trash. In some locations, it rolls inland as far as 10 km (6 mi).

Loss of life and property is astonishing. The tsunami damages or destroys roads, railways, a dam, and more than 125,000 buildings. Property damage may be more than $300 billion. More than 5,300 people are injured, and more than 23,300 are dead or missing. Most of the damage and casualties are the result of the tsunami.

The huge 9.0 magnitude earthquake off Japan's northeastern coast on March 11, 2011, created a massive tsunami that washed over the low-lying coastal land. This image of the Sendai Airport shows cars and airplanes strewn in the wake of the huge wave.

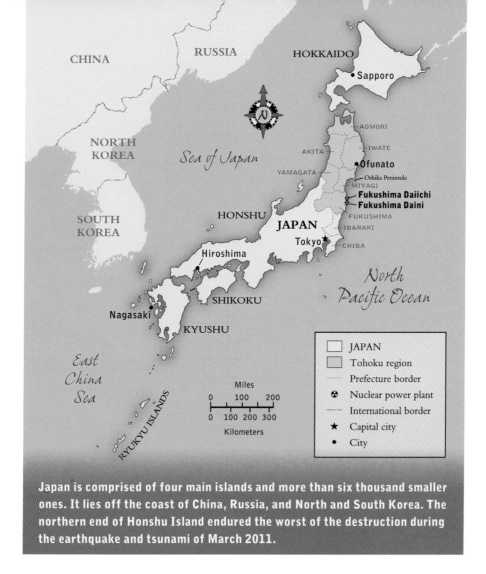

Japan is comprised of four main islands and more than six thousand smaller ones. It lies off the coast of China, Russia, and North and South Korea. The northern end of Honshu Island endured the worst of the destruction during the earthquake and tsunami of March 2011.

PREPARATION SAVES LIVES

The Tohoku quake is extremely powerful, registering 9.0 on the Richter scale (the most common measurement of earthquake intensity). Only four earthquakes since 1900 have released more energy. Yet the loss of life in Japan, though large, was much less than in serious quakes in other parts of the world.

For example, the 7.0 earthquake that struck Haiti in 2010 released only a thousandth as much energy and did not cause a tsunami. Yet it was more than ten times as deadly. More than three hundred thousand people died.

In 2005 a 9.1 earthquake under the Indian Ocean, near Aceh on the northern tip of Sumatra, Indonesia, triggered a tsunami similar to the one that struck Tohoku. The Aceh tsunami was also ten times as deadly as Tohoku. It killed more than 230,000 people on Sumatra, on other Indonesian islands, and in neighboring countries.

Why do so many fewer people die in Japan? Two words: preparation and warning. The Japanese are the most prepared people in the world when earthquakes and tsunamis strike. And they have warning systems that alert them in time to seek safety.

Most of the Haitian deaths were caused by collapsing buildings. In Japan most of the buildings survive the earthquake with little or no damage. But even where buildings suffer damage, most people escape injury because of Japan's earthquake warning system.

Meanwhile, out in the ocean, a system of undersea sensors and floating communication buoys called DART (Deep-ocean Assessment and Reporting of Tsunamis) detects the early signs of a tsunami. It takes nine minutes to collect and compare enough readings. Then DART sends a warning to a communications satellite, which relays the message to a receiver on the ground.

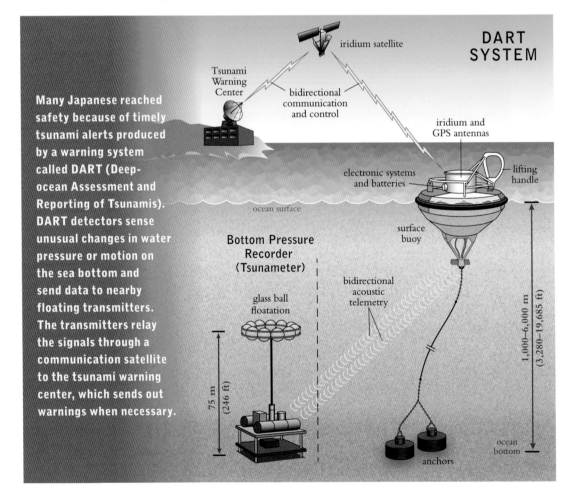

Many Japanese reached safety because of timely tsunami alerts produced by a warning system called DART (Deep-ocean Assessment and Reporting of Tsunamis). DART detectors sense unusual changes in water pressure or motion on the sea bottom and send data to nearby floating transmitters. The transmitters relay the signals through a communication satellite to the tsunami warning center, which sends out warnings when necessary.

DART SYSTEM

iridium satellite

Tsunami Warning Center

bidirectional communication and control

iridium and GPS antennas

electronic systems and batteries

lifting handle

ocean surface

surface buoy

Bottom Pressure Recorder (Tsunameter)

bidirectional acoustic telemetry

glass ball floatation

75 m (246 ft)

1,000–6,000 m (3,280–19,685 ft)

ocean bottom

anchors

In the hardest-hit areas, the tsunami alerts arrive about fifteen minutes ahead of the deadly wave. That isn't much time, but the Japanese people respond quickly when tsunami warning sirens blare. Many cities and towns, such as the fishing village of Ofunato in Iwate Prefecture, have clearly marked escape routes with signs in Japanese and in English. Tens of thousands of Tohoku inhabitants lose their homes but escape to higher ground.

How Earthquake Warning Systems Work

Japan's earthquake warning system uses ground-motion detectors called seismometers. The system takes advantage of the fact that every earthquake sends out two kinds of vibrations. These are called primary and secondary waves, or P-waves and S-waves.

The P-waves are sound waves with such a low pitch that they can be felt but not heard. They pass through Earth without causing damage. They often go unnoticed. They are called primary because they travel faster and arrive first. As soon as a seismometer senses a P-wave, it sends out an alert. Before the damaging secondary waves arrive, people get messages on cell phones, televisions, and special radios that turn on automatically.

People in Miyagi Prefecture (above) had very little time to react to the earthquake warning. This photo shows some of the destruction there two days afterward.

Cities and towns closest to the epicenter get the least warning. In the Great Tohoku Earthquake, the coast of Miyagi Prefecture near Oshika has only about ten seconds between the alert and the shaking. People in Tokyo, 370 km (230 mi) from the epicenter, have nearly a minute to take action. People on the lower floors of buildings get out. Doctors stop surgeries. People get out of elevators. Drivers move their cars to the roadside.

Ofunato:
One Town's Tsunami Story

From the hills overlooking the ocean, residents of the northern Iwate fishing village of Ofunato can do nothing but watch as the tsunami enters the narrow coastal valley leading to their town. Squeezed between the hills, it grows higher and higher.

It enters the town and surges past signs marking tsunami escape routes. It wipes out homes and businesses. It quickly submerges a stone marker that indicates the high point of the last tsunami in 1960 and keeps on going.

Some people who live above that marker think they are safe. By the time they realize they are wrong, it is too late to escape. Hundreds drown.

The tsunami wiped out this residential town on Japan's northeastern coast. The earthquake and subsequent tsunami left at least 23,300 dead or missing and hundreds of thousands homeless.

But most Ofunato residents scramble to the safety of higher ground. When international teams of rescue workers finally arrive, five days have passed. Their bulldozers clear a pathway back into town. Where hundreds of homes once stood, survivors find only a few traces of their old life—perhaps a favorite rice bowl or a traditional Japanese robe that once belonged to a deceased ancestor.

But they are grateful to be alive. With the help of the recovery teams, they begin the difficult task of cleanup and rebuilding.

By late July, the town is showing a few signs of normality. The village's huge tugboat still sits in someone's backyard where the great wave deposited it. But the fish market has reopened. The smaller boats, now repaired, are setting off for monthlong fishing trips.

Ofunato is coming back to life.

The force of the tsunami lifted this tugboat ashore in the town of Ofunato.

MELTDOWN!
WHEN PREPARATION IS NOT ENOUGH

As the news from Tohoku spreads around the world, many people immediately draw comparisons to Aceh and Haiti. Despite the huge estimates of property damage and human casualties, the rest of the world praises Japanese engineering and preparation.

But within a day, very bad news arrives from Fukushima Prefecture, just south of Miyagi. The Tokyo Electric Power Company (TEPCO) operates two large nuclear power plants there, along the coast. The Fukushima Daiichi (Japanese for "number 1") plant in the towns of Okuma and Futaba has six reactors. Fukushima Daini (number 2), in Nahara and Tomioka, has four.

When the earthquake alert goes out, the Fukushima reactors shut down automatically. They stop generating electricity. But they still need water to keep the fuel in their central regions (their cores) from overheating. Large electric pumps must circulate water to keep them from melting down.

THE EMERGENCY BEGINS

The pumps usually draw electricity from outside the plants. But the earthquake and tsunami knock out power stations all over the region. So the pumps at both Fukushima plants switch to backup power. For a short time, it comes from large batteries. The batteries are good for only a few hours. So the stations also have emergency backup diesel generators in case the main power is still out.

At Fukushima Daini, the backup generators kick in as they are supposed to. The reactors there will be safe. But at Fukushima Daiichi, something is terribly wrong. The tsunami has flooded and knocked out the backup generators. Reactors 4, 5, and 6 are shut down for maintenance. But if the other three reactors lose their cooling, they will suffer one of the most serious kinds of nuclear accidents—a core meltdown.

The batteries will last for only a few hours. Before they run out, the nuclear engineers will have to come up with an emergency plan to prevent not just one meltdown but three!

No one yet realizes it, but the earthquake has damaged reactor 1 so badly that it is already melting down. Despite frantic and heroic efforts by TEPCO workers and engineers, reactors 2 and 3 will follow. Also

The earthquake damaged reactors at the Fukushima Daiichi nuclear power plant. Water for cooling the reactor core boiled off, causing temperatures to rise dramatically. The intense heat led to explosions in two of the reactors, where fire broke out. Damaged reactor 3 is shown here on March 16, 2011. Unmanned aerial drones were sent to photograph the damage.

in the coming days, two serious explosions and several small fires will spread harmful radioactive material for miles.

Fukushima Daiichi workers and nearby residents will soon be exposed to dangerous radiation that could shorten their lives. Tens of thousands of people will have to leave their homes for months or even years. Farmers will have to destroy their crops or milk. Fishers will worry about the safety of their catch. Factories and businesses all over Japan will have to shut down because they do not have enough electric power.

Because of the nuclear emergency, people soon stop comparing the Tohoku disaster to the Haiti earthquake and Aceh tsunami. Instead, Fukushima 2011 is linked with two other serious nuclear accidents: Three Mile Island (TMI) in Pennsylvania in 1979 and Chernobyl, Ukraine, in 1986.

Chapter 2

ENERGY
FROM THE
HEART OF MATTER

What is a nuclear meltdown, and why is it so dangerous? The answer to those questions begins deep in the heart of matter.

ATOMS AND NUCLEI

Every substance on Earth is made of atoms. The central part of an atom, called the nucleus, contains most of its matter. It is made up of two different kinds of particles called protons and neutrons. Surrounding the nucleus are very light particles called electrons.

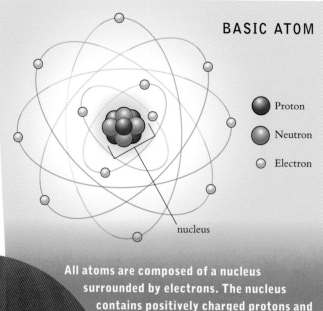

BASIC ATOM

- Proton
- Neutron
- Electron

nucleus

All atoms are composed of a nucleus surrounded by electrons. The nucleus contains positively charged protons and uncharged neutrons, bound together by a powerful nuclear force. The electrons carry a negative charge.

British physicist J. J. Thomson (1856–1940) won the 1906 Nobel Prize in Physics for his discovery of the subatomic particle known as the electron in 1897. He is shown here in his lab.

A proton and an electron each carry the same amount of electric charge. But their charges are of opposite types. Protons carry positive charge, and electrons carry negative charge. Neutrons are electrically neutral. They are just slightly heavier than protons. Together, protons and neutrons are called nucleons.

The number of protons determines the type of substance, or element, the atom is. All hydrogen atoms have only 1 proton. All helium atoms have 2 protons. Oxygen has 8, iron has 26, lead has 82, and uranium has 92 protons.

An atom has the same number of electrons as protons, so its total charge is zero. Electrical charges of the same type repel, or push each other apart. Opposite charges attract. The closer two electrically charged particles are to one another, the stronger the force is between them.

Electrical attraction binds negative electrons to their positive nuclei. It also holds atoms together to make molecules.

RADIOACTIVITY

Between 1896 and 1898, scientists discovered mysterious rays of energy coming from uranium and other kinds of atoms. They called those atoms radioactive. Over the next several years, scientists made many important discoveries about radioactivity and the inner workings of atoms. They discovered three kinds of radioactivity that they named after the first three letters of the Greek alphabet—alpha, beta, and gamma.

Another important finding was that an element can have atoms with different masses. These are called isotopes. We now know that different isotopes of the same element have the same numbers of protons but different numbers of neutrons. For instance, in natural uranium, 99.3 percent of the nuclei have 146 neutrons. Along with its 92 protons, this element has a total of 238 nucleons (U-238). Most other uranium nuclei have 143 neutrons (U-235).

When the nucleus was discovered in 1911, scientists were astonished at how small it is—only about one hundred thousandth the diameter of the atom itself. They wondered how that could be possible. With so much positive charge crammed into such a small space, why doesn't a powerful electric force push the protons apart?

The answer is that there is a powerful nuclear force that attracts nucleons to each other. It is so strong that it overwhelms the electrical repulsion between protons. Physicists call that the strong nuclear force.

The strong nuclear force is connected to alpha radiation. All alpha radiation is made up of particles with two protons and two neutrons—helium nuclei. It takes a lot of energy to hold a large nucleus together. Sometimes an alpha particle escapes a radioactive nucleus, such as uranium, and takes some of that energy with it.

Imagine how much energy would be released if that nucleus ever split apart altogether! That splitting is called nuclear fission, and you don't have to imagine it. It actually happens naturally to some radioactive nuclei including U-235. It also happens to the most common isotope of plutonium, Pu-239.

Beginning in 1942 and continuing until the end of World War II (1939-1945), a group of American scientists and engineers worked on a way to produce fission in huge numbers of nuclei in a very short time. The result is a short but powerful blast of energy—a bomb. On August 6, 1945, the United States dropped a U-235 bomb on the Japanese city of Hiroshima. Three days later, they dropped a Pu-239 bomb on Nagasaki, Japan.

The two bombs caused horrible damage, and they ended the war. The Japanese surrendered on August 15, 1945.

After the war, many of the bomb scientists saw a way to use nuclear energy in a peaceful way. They could use it to create steam to drive an electric generator.

The age of nuclear power had begun.

Survivors walk through the decimated streets of Nagasaki, Japan, after the United States dropped an atomic bomb on the city on August 9, 1945, to bring an end to World War II.

Lise Meitner and the Discovery of Nuclear Fission

When authors tell the story of radioactivity, they always mention the great woman physicist Marie Curie (1867–1934). But Lise Meitner (1878–1968), another pioneering woman physicist, gets much less attention. She was one of the discoverers of nuclear fission.

Lise Meitner was born in Vienna, Austria, at a time when girls' public education ended at the age of 14. Still, she went to the University of Vienna and earned a doctoral degree with the highest possible honors.

Even that was not enough to get her a job as a scientist. So her friend Otto Hahn persuaded an institute director at the University of Berlin (Germany) to let her work on radioactivity in a converted carpenter's shop with an outside entrance. She was not allowed into the rest of the building. When other scientists greeted her and Hahn together, they usually said only, "Guten Tag, Herr Hahn!" (Good day, Mr. Hahn!)

Lise Meitner and Otto Hahn are shown here in the laboratory of the Kaiser Wilhelm Institute in Berlin (Germany) in 1925. Meitner and Hahn discovered nuclear fission, the technology that led to the later development of nuclear weapons and nuclear power.

Meitner *(standing third from left)*, Hahn *(standing center)*, and other well-known scientists of the time gathered in Munster, Germany, for a tea during the 1932 Bunsentagung, an international conference on physics.

Times changed, and by 1919 Meitner became probably the first woman in Germany to earn the title professor. Things went well for her until the mid-1930s, when Adolf Hitler and the Nazis came to power and began a campaign to eliminate Jews from important positions. This even included people like Meitner, who were born Jewish and converted to Christianity.

In 1938, with Hahn's help, Meitner escaped to Sweden. Soon after her arrival, she got a letter from Hahn that described some very curious laboratory results.

While cross-country skiing with her nephew, Otto Frisch, who was visiting from Denmark, she described the results. They came up with the thought that uranium nuclei might be splitting apart. They stopped to make some calculations, then got back on their skis. They continued talking physics as they enjoyed the snow. By the time they returned, they had a full explanation of Hahn's results: nuclear fission.

FROM BOMBS TO POWER PLANTS

Nuclear bombs and power plants work because certain isotopes of certain elements undergo fission. What makes them fissionable while other isotopes are not? The answer is in the way the strong nuclear force works.

The strong nuclear force has a short range. That means it is effective only when the protons and neutrons are very close together. Only certain arrangements of protons and neutrons hold together to form nuclei.

Inside a nucleus, protons and neutrons are constantly rearranging themselves. In the nucleus of a fissionable isotope, by chance, they sometimes regroup into two smaller nuclei with a few neutrons left over.

Those smaller positively charged nuclei repel each other electrically. That blows the nucleus apart. The smaller nuclei are called fission products. The extra neutrons go flying off with great energy.

For any one nucleus, fission is very rare. In a piece of natural uranium, it takes 710 million years for half of the original U-235 nuclei to undergo fission. Scientists call that time the half-life.

U-238 is much more stable than its slightly smaller cousin. It occasionally produces alpha particles, but it never undergoes fission. Its half-life is 4.5 billion years.

CRITICAL MASS AND CHAIN REACTIONS

How can we get usable energy from radioactivity if most nuclei don't decay for hundreds of millions of years? The trick is to create a chain reaction.

For example, suppose a U-235 nucleus undergoes fission and one of its neutrons is captured by another U-235 nucleus. The second nucleus becomes the very unstable isotope U-236. Almost immediately, the U-236 undergoes fission, sending off its own high-speed neutrons. If another U-235 nucleus captures one of those neutrons, it undergoes fission and produces still more neutrons.

In a chain reaction, one nuclear fission quickly follows another. Soon most of the U-235 nuclei are gone. That releases an enormous amount of energy in a very short time.

Natural uranium does not produce a chain reaction. Its U-235 nuclei are so rare that when one of them undergoes fission, the neutrons produced almost always escape or are captured by U-238 nuclei.

Creating a chain reaction requires making "enriched" uranium, which has more U-235 than natural uranium. Reactor fuel has three to

The United States tested nuclear bombs in Alamogordo, New Mexico, in 1945 as part of a project that was code-named Trinity. This nuclear explosion shows the great amount of energy that can be released in a chain reaction. The fuel in a nuclear reactor cannot explode, but it releases enormous amounts of energy in a controlled way.

four times as much U-235 as natural uranium. That means 2 to 3 percent of its atoms are U-235.

Weapons-grade uranium is enriched even more. A fission bomb explodes when it has enough fissionable nuclei in one place. The necessary amount is called a critical mass. With less mass than that, too few fission neutrons set off another fission, and the chain reaction dies.

A nuclear blast is very destructive. But that is not the only harm the bomb does. It also spreads highly radioactive fission products over a wide area. Some fission products are especially hazardous when they get into food or the water supply. Certain isotopes of iodine, cesium, and strontium can endanger human health for years.

Plutonium itself can be very poisonous, especially if a person inhales or swallows small particles. A uranium bomb or reactor produces Pu-239 from the U-238 nuclei in the fuel.

CHAIN REACTIONS IN NUCLEAR REACTORS

The fuel in a nuclear power plant is not rich enough in fissionable nuclei to explode. Like natural uranium, reactor grade fuel can never be made into a bomb. Its fissionable nuclei are too spread out to keep a chain reaction going.

Yet nuclear reactors depend on creating a chain reaction. How is that possible? The trick is to slow down the fission neutrons by adding a substance called a moderator.

When a fast-moving neutron passes by a fissionable nucleus, it doesn't get captured unless it is nearly on course for a direct hit. Since the nucleus is about a hundred thousandth the size of its atom, most fission neutrons zip right by.

A neutron that passes through a moderator slows down. That means it takes longer to pass each atom. With more time to act, the strong force of the nucleus has greater influence. So adding a moderator makes neutron capture, fission, and a chain reaction possible.

TURNING FISSION ENERGY INTO ELECTRICITY

Some nuclear reactors use graphite (a form of pure carbon) as a moderator. But most commercial reactors use water. The water not only moderates the neutrons but also absorbs the great heat of the reactions. It is called the cooling water because it keeps the temperature of the reactor core under control.

Despite its name, the cooling water becomes extremely hot as it absorbs the core's heat. It then leaves the core and enters a system of pipes and pumps. The pipes carry it to a heat exchanger as either superheated steam or as extremely hot water kept from boiling by high pressure. (If the reactor uses superheated steam, it is called a boiling water reactor. If it uses hot water under pressure, it is called a pressurized water reactor.)

The heat exchanger transfers heat from a loop of pipes containing the cooling water to another loop

Fuel rods hold uranium or plutonium pellets that give off heat as they undergo fission. This spent (used up) fuel rod has been removed from a reactor and is being placed underwater in a storage pool. The rod still contains dangerous radioactive material that needs to be stored and disposed of carefully.

that circulates water drawn from a nearby lake or stream. In that second loop, the heat turns the water into the steam that drives the generator. Then the cooling water goes back into the core.

Water vapor rises out of the top of a cooling tower at a nuclear power plant in Pennsylvania.

The two loops are kept separate. Only heat, not water, passes between them.

Reactor fuel is usually in the form of rods—closed cylinders about 4 m (13 ft) long and made of a zirconium alloy (a metal that does not corrode easily yet allows neutrons to pass through it). Inside the rods are pellets of uranium (or plutonium) oxide.

Fuel rods are bundled together in the reactor core. Between the fuel bundles are a small number of control rods. Control rods are made of materials that absorb neutrons. They can slow down or even stop a chain reaction.

Strong springs at the top of the reactor core, along with gravity, push the control rods into the core. The reactor can produce power only when powerful electromagnets pull the control rods upward away from the fuel rods.

The design of nuclear reactors makes nuclear explosions impossible. At the first sign of trouble, the control rods spring into the core. Even if that fails, an overheating reactor would lose its moderator. Water pipes would burst or graphite would burn.

Without a moderator, the chain reaction ends. But stopping a chain reaction is not enough to make a reactor safe. Reactors have to be designed to protect people from radioactivity in the fuel and fission products even when serious problems occur.

The most serious kind of reactor accident leads to a meltdown. That kind of failure threatens people, property—and even the future of the nuclear power industry itself.

Chapter 3

NUCLEAR REACTOR *SUCCESSES* AND FAILURES

In the years following World War II, demand for electricity grew at an amazing rate. And it looked as if it would continue to grow that fast for decades to come. The people who ran electric companies began to worry about getting enough coal or oil for their generators. Could the world run out of coal or oil? Would the countries with the greatest supplies be able to control the world by controlling these fuels?

"I'd never go back *from Electricity* to old-fashioned cooking now!"

Electric cookers have thermostat control on the oven, quick-heating boiling plates, and new, variable switches which give perfect heat-control from fast boiling to slow simmering—*and lower*, if you want it!

Go round and see one at your Electricity Service Centre. They are friendly, knowledgeable people there, and will be glad to help you. They can also let you have details about easy payments, and the new, free book, full of clever ideas for saving work, ELECTRICITY IN YOUR KITCHEN: or you are welcome to write for a copy to EDA, 2 Savoy Hill, London, W.C.2.

ELECTRICITY *a Power of Good* *for cooking!* AND FOR WATER-HEATING TOO!

This ad from 1953 touts the joys and conveniences of cooking on an electric stove. The introduction of new electric gadgets and household appliances in the 1950s upped the demand for electricity in the industrialized world. Some energy companies turned to nuclear power to supply electricity affordably.

Nuclear energy looked like the best way to deal with those concerns. In 1958 the world's first commercial nuclear power plant went into operation at Shippingport, Pennsylvania, about 50 km (30 mi) northwest of Pittsburgh. People who lived in the Pittsburgh area at that time, including the author, remember the news reports: the power plant produced so much energy from so little fuel that electricity would someday be "too cheap to meter."

As is often the case with a new technology, nuclear power didn't live up to all its promises. Nuclear accidents could be dangerous, so people demanded strong safety regulations. The industry also had to deal with environmental concerns. For example, as the reactor creates fissions for energy, the amount of radioactive fission products in the fuel rods increases. When the rods are used up, how and where should they be disposed of?

For almost twenty years after Shippingport opened, most people didn't worry about such questions. They were confident in the nuclear power industry. Then came the meltdown at Three Mile Island (TMI).

MELTDOWN IN THE SUSQUEHANNA

Three Mile Island sits in the beautiful, broad Susquehanna River, 18 km (11 mi) downstream from Pennsylvania's capital city of Harrisburg. There, in the early 1970s, the Babcock & Wilcox (B&W) Company built two pressurized water reactors for the General Public Utilities (GPU) Corporation.

B&W had built similar reactors at many sites, including the Davis-Besse plant on the shore of Lake Erie just east of Toledo, Ohio. The B&W design met all the standards set by the U.S. Nuclear Regulatory Commission (NRC).

The meltdown at TMI might never have occurred if the operators there had known about a serious problem at Davis-Besse in September 1977. Two things went wrong there, and together, they almost caused the loss of the plant. The first was a bad indicator on the control panel. It was supposed to tell them when the water level was getting low in the core. It was unnoticed until the second problem occurred: a stuck valve.

This particular valve prevented cooling water pipes from bursting if the pressure got too high. It would open automatically and then close after releasing enough cooling water to relieve the pressure. On that day at Davis-Besse, it got stuck in the open position. Cooling water continued to flow out of the core.

This aerial photo from 1979 shows the four cooling towers at Three Mile Island, on the Susquehanna River in Pennsylvania. A similar reactor in Toledo, Ohio, experienced a system failure that nearly caused a meltdown. A year and a half later, Three Mile Island went through the same chain of events, this time ending in a meltdown.

Without enough cooling water, the core temperature began to rise. An automatic backup cooling system went into action. It began spraying the core with emergency cooling water. That was when the indicator problem became important. Alarms went off. But fooled by the bad indicator, the operators thought the core still had plenty of water. So they turned off the emergency coolant.

With the stuck valve still releasing cooling water and with no water flowing into the core, the stage was set for a core meltdown. Fortunately, Mike Derivan, a highly trained shift supervisor, was on duty. He figured out what was happening. The rapidly rising temperature told him the core had to be losing coolant no matter what the indicator showed. "Shut the block valve!" he shouted. The emergency was over. The entire incident lasted only an hour.

A WARNING TOO LATE

B&W was slow reporting the near-miss at Davis-Besse to the NRC. It took eighteen months, until March 21, 1979, before the NRC finally ordered an investigation.

That was too late. A week later, at four in the morning of March 28, 1979, a pressure relief valve stuck open in the core-cooling loop at TMI reactor 2. This time, the plant was at a higher power level than Davis-Besse had been. This time, it took sixteen hours before someone figured out the problem.

By the time the valve was closed, the upper two-thirds of the core was destroyed. And so much cooling water escaped that it overflowed the radioactive waste storage tanks.

That overflow released some radioactivity into the atmosphere, but not enough to be alarming. On March 29, GPU announced that the worst was over. But in fact, a terrifying event was just beginning.

The melted zirconium of fuel rods had reached 1200°C (2200°F). At that temperature, zirconium reacts chemically with the water to produce highly explosive hydrogen gas. By late on March 30, a bubble of hydrogen was growing inside the core.

The hydrogen wasn't mixing with air, so it was not likely to explode. Even so, the bubble meant trouble for the reactor core. The bigger it grew, the less cooling water reached the core. With less cooling, the meltdown could resume. This time it might melt through the steel surrounding the core. Melted fuel with its fission products could get into the soil. From there, underground water could spread it throughout the region.

Pennsylvania officials rushed to make evacuation plans. Governor Richard Thornburgh urged pregnant women and pre-school children within 8 km (5 mi) of TMI to leave. Many others—about one hundred thousand people altogether—were concerned enough to leave their homes.

An indicator failure and a valve malfunction in this reactor at the Three Mile Island nuclear power plant combined to produce a meltdown in March 1979.

After the nuclear accident at Three Mile Island, residents near the plant were evacuated for safety reasons. These people, gathered in a sports arena in early April 1979, sought to be relocated temporarily.

Engineers solved the bubble problem quickly, and the crisis passed. It took a few weeks after that for the reactor to cool enough to be considered stable. Radioactivity measurements showed that no one outside the reactor complex had been exposed to more than minor amounts of excess radiation.

TRAGEDY AT CHERNOBYL

At first, the meltdown at TMI slowed the nuclear power industry. But since the accident did not harm people or the environment, people's confidence in nuclear power began to recover. That recovery ended seven years later with the worst nuclear disaster in history. It happened at the Chernobyl nuclear power complex in Ukraine, then one of fifteen republics of the Soviet Union.

The nuclear reactors at Chernobyl used graphite as the moderator. Cooling water flowed through the reactor core in pipes. The reactors did not have steel reactor vessels to contain the fuel and control rods. Only concrete containment buildings protected the environment in case of a meltdown. The lack of a reactor vessel is one of two reasons that most countries do not approve Chernobyl-type reactors.

The second reason is that without cooling water to absorb some of the neutrons, the chain reactions become more intense. The reactor power increases until the graphite ignites in a fiery nonnuclear explosion.

The Soviet government was more concerned with electricity for economic growth than with safety. The Chernobyl reactor design was cheaper and easier to build. And its designers insisted it could be operated safely. Those designers did not anticipate a very bad decision by reactor operators. On April 25, 1986, the operators decided to test a safety system while the reactor ran at one-fifth full power. A Soviet nuclear scientist described the experiment as "like airline pilots experimenting with the engines in flight."

To keep the reactor running smoothly during the test, the operators had to slow down the cooling water. The slower the cooling water flowed, the more time it spent within the core, and the hotter it got. Suddenly, it was hot enough to boil.

The rapid boiling reduced the amount of water in the core. With less cooling, the power surged and increased the boiling still more. The reactor was out of control.

An operator pushed an emergency button to insert the control rods, but it was too late. A meltdown began. The graphite moderator burst into flame. Explosions tore open the plant's side and roof. They even cracked the core's thousand-ton concrete lid.

It took nearly two weeks to bring the fires under control. By then, thirty-one people, mostly firefighters, were dead or dying of radiation poisoning. The explosion released more radioactive material than the World War II Hiroshima and Nagasaki atomic bombs combined. Radioactive smoke and dust spread across Earth's Northern Hemisphere.

This photo of the Chernobyl nuclear power complex in Ukraine shows the destruction after an explosion rocked the plant's fourth reactor *(foreground)* in April 1986.

Thousands of people in Ukraine and elsewhere in northern Europe developed cancer from the radioactivity. The radiation also led to birth defects in thousands of babies. The town of Pripyat, where the Chernobyl power plant workers lived, and the area around it had to be abandoned. People will not be able to live there safely for decades.

Yet despite the horrors, Chernobyl was only a minor setback for the nuclear industry. Everyone knew that an accident like that would never happen with water-moderated reactors. Everyone knew that reactor operators would never again try such a risky test. Everyone knew that at TMI, even though so much had gone wrong, almost no radioactivity was released into the environment.

By 2011 the nuclear power industry was growing rapidly around the world. Then came Fukushima.

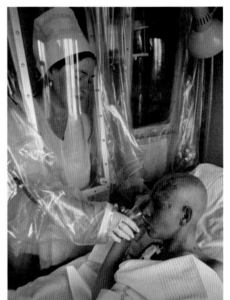

After Chernobyl many people developed cancer, such as this man. In the twenty-first century, scientists continue to study the long-term impact of the nuclear disaster, which spread radiation over much of northern Europe.

Many towns, such as Pripyat, Ukraine, were evacuated after the Chernobyl disaster and remain ghost towns. This photo shows an abandoned kindergarten in Pripyat.

A Governor's Crisis

On March 28, 1979, Richard L. Thornburgh had been governor of Pennsylvania for only seventy-two days. He was having a breakfast meeting when an aide interrupted.

"I was called out of the meeting to take a call from our emergency management director at about 7:50 A.M. And the report from him was that there had been an accident at the Three Mile Island Nuclear Plant," Thornburgh recalled in a newspaper interview thirty years later.

He knew right away that "this was a matter of some consequence." But making decisions about what to do and how to inform the public was a challenge. "The principal difficulty we had was getting at the facts and determining precisely what happened. . . . [T]he utility [company]was not terribly forthcoming. . . . And a variety of so-called experts were offering advice to the public. It was a pretty chaotic situation," he recalled.

Part of the confusion was that the public didn't understand the difference between a meltdown and a bomb. TMI was not going to disappear in a mushroom cloud. But the governor understood that a meltdown was a serious threat to human health and the environment. His effort to explain what residents faced was complicated by a popular motion picture. "*The China Syndrome* was playing in the area," he said. "I remember vividly one line in that movie where one of the physicists was describing the nature of the damage that would be done. They said it would permanently contaminate an area the size of the state of Pennsylvania."

Over the next few days, the governor's confident yet serious manner prevented panic even when he had to ask people to evacuate. When the reactor was stabilized and everyone had returned safely home, the new governor had won the respect of Pennsylvania and the nation for the way he handled the crisis.

U.S. president Jimmy Carter and his wife, Rosalynn *(center)*, visit the Three Mile Island Plant shortly after the nuclear disaster there. Pennsylvania governor Richard L. Thornburgh *(wearing glasses)* stands next to the president.

Chapter 4

WHAT WENT WRONG AT *FUKUSHIMA?*

What exactly happened at Fukushima? And how can we prevent an event like that from happening again? Those are the most important questions facing the public and the future of nuclear power after the Great Tohoku Earthquake and tsunami.

They are also very difficult to answer. Let's begin by looking at the Fukushima meltdowns day by day.

ON THE SCENE OF A DISASTER

MARCH 11, 2011: On the day of the earthquake, Fukushima Daiichi reactor 1 is one of the oldest nuclear reactors in Japan. It has been in operation since 1971. It probably should be replaced, but TEPCO wants to get as much use out of it as possible.

At 2:46 P.M., the shaking starts. Strong earthquakes are common in Japan, so the plant has been built to withstand a jolt at least as large as 8.5 on the Richter scale. But this earthquake measures 9.0.

When the earthquake alarm sounds, reactor 1 workers head for the exits. On the way out, a twenty-seven-year-old maintenance engineer senses trouble.

"I personally saw pipes that came apart," he tells a reporter later. "There's no doubt that the earthquake did a lot of damage inside the plant."

A technician in his late thirties

The tsunami in Japan washed away a warehouse and vehicles in a coastal town in Miyagi Prefecture, leaving a road covered with a mountain of debris. It took workers nearly three months to clear the road.

recognizes the first signs of a meltdown. "I could see that several pipes had cracked open, including what I believe were cold water supply pipes," he recalls in an interview. "That would mean that coolant couldn't get to the reactor core."

Though TEPCO doesn't know it yet, the technician is right. Reactor 1 is in deep trouble. It is losing cooling water. Its core will soon begin melting down, and no one will be able to do anything to save it.

Meanwhile, in reactor 2, the first shaking makes Horoyuki Kohno pause. He's not even sure it is an earthquake. It could be a minor turbine problem. Then the building shudders and warning sirens blare. He and his fellow workers hurry out as parts of the ceiling crash around them. The core of the nearly thirty-six-year-old reactor is not damaged.

Outside, Kohno's coworkers are "shouting about a tsunami. At that point, I really thought I might die," he recalls. Instead of going to their cars, the workers are heading for the safety of upper floors of buildings or higher ground.

From the top of a small hill, Kohno sees black smoke coming from the reactors. That's a good sign. It is the exhaust of the large backup diesel generators that pump cooling water when the outside electricity fails. As long as that water flows, there will not be a meltdown.

The early indications are also good in the power plant operations

As **TEPCO** workers desperately tried to avoid a meltdown at the Fukushima plant, members of Japan's self-defense force evacuated people *(above)* from towns devastated by the tsunami.

center. In the first minute of the quake, the control rods drop into all the reactor cores. That stops the chain reactions. At 3:27 P.M., the first wave of the tsunami slams into the 10 m (33 ft) seawall. At a little higher than 4 m (13 ft), it causes no problem.

But behind it is a monster. At 3:35 P.M., a 15 m (50 ft) wave rolls over the barrier. It tosses cars around like bathtub toys and heads for the reactors. It knocks out the backup generators and washes away their fuel tanks.

By 3:52 P.M., the workers in the control room fear the worst for reactor 2. Their whiteboard is filled with notes about the growing crisis. They add "ECCS injection not possible" to the list. That means water is not flowing from its Emergency Core Cooling System. To keep the core from melting down, TEPCO workers hurry to find a way to replace water as it boils off. They start spraying the core with high-pressure hoses to keep it cool.

MARCH 12, 2011: Things are only slightly better for reactor 3. Its emergency batteries keep the cooling-water pumps operating until their power runs out. Early on the morning after the quake, those batteries die. The flow of cooling water stops, and evaporation begins. Ninety minutes later, the fuel rods are no longer completely under water. Workers are now spraying two cores at once, desperately trying to prevent meltdowns.

TEPCO still doesn't know how serious the leaks are at reactor 1. In fact, its core has already almost completely melted. The hot zirconium alloy is beginning to react with water to produce hydrogen. But unlike at TMI, the hydrogen is mixing with air. At 3:36 P.M., one day and fifty minutes after the earthquake, a powerful explosion brings down the concrete building around reactor 1.

Radioactivity is escaping into the air. To stop more from getting into the environment, TEPCO brings in fire trucks to pump seawater onto reactor 1's core.

MARCH 13–15, 2011: Early on March 13, the high-pressure spray system for reactor 3 stops working. By 9:00 A.M., its core begins to melt. On the morning of March 14, its building explodes. By 3:00 P.M., most of its fuel has melted to the bottom of the reactor vessel.

The March 14 explosion at reactor 3 damages the water supply for reactor 2. By 1:15 P.M. that day, that spray stops completely. At 8:00 P.M., the reactor begins melting down. A day later, its meltdown is also complete.

But that is not the end of the trouble at Fukushima Daiichi.

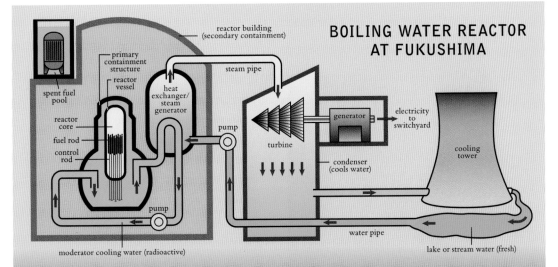

This diagram shows a boiling water reactor like the three that melted down at Fukushima Daiichi. One loop of water is pumped through the reactor core where it absorbs the heat from a controlled nuclear chain reaction and boils. Under high pressure, the steam gets very hot. It enters a pipe that carries it to a heat exchanger. The outside of that pipe becomes hot enough to boil water in a second loop. That creates steam to drive an electric generator. The meltdowns occurred when the pumps lost power and the heat in the reactor core could not be transferred away.

TROUBLE FROM SPENT FUEL RODS

One of the problems of nuclear power is what to do with the spent fuel rods—rods that are no longer useful. They haven't used up all their U-235, but they have enough fission products to spoil the chain reaction. They also contain plutonium.

Most reactors store spent fuel in water-filled pools. The rods stay under water for many years until the radioactivity from the fission products has died down. Heat from that radioactivity makes water evaporate from those pools, so it has to be replaced constantly. If the spent fuel pool goes dry, the rods can catch fire.

Fukushima Daiichi has six spent fuel pools, one for each reactor. While TEPCO workers are busy fighting three meltdowns, they also have to worry about water for spent fuel pools at all six reactors. The pools for reactors 3 and 4 are the most troublesome. They may be leaking. Military helicopters dump giant buckets of seawater onto these storage pools to keep them from going dry.

Firefighters gather to douse overheated reactors with water at the Fukushima Daiichi nuclear power plant on March 18, 2011, one week after the earthquake and tsunami hit Japan.

EVACUATION AND ROLLING BLACKOUT

Meanwhile, the Japanese government declares an evacuation zone. They urge everyone living within 20 km (12 mi) of Fukushima Daiichi to leave as soon as possible. Government workers have detected radiation levels in that area that put people's health in serious jeopardy.

Tap water in the area is too radioactive for infants to drink. Farmers have to destroy vegetables and milk contaminated with radioactivity. Seafood in coastal waters is also contaminated from the overflow of radioactive water from storage tanks.

Besides people in the area that immediately surrounds the reactors, the rest of Japan faces electric

Officials wear protective gear to scan evacuated people in Koriyama, Japan, for radiation levels. This city is about thirty minutes from the Fukushima power plant.

power shortages right after the earthquake and tsunami. Other Japanese nuclear plants shut down as a precaution.

People and businesses lose power periodically as TEPCO and other companies schedule rolling electrical blackouts to share the burden the best way they can. Many manufacturers have to shut down. All over the world, automobile companies and dealers face shortages of important parts.

In late April, the Japanese government makes it illegal to stay in the evacuation zone. It takes weeks before normal electric service is restored.

Step by step, TEPCO begins bringing the situation at Fukushima under control. But it is a long process to reach "cold shutdown," where the core is cool enough that the meltdown will not begin again.

By midsummer 2011, officials can see that cold shutdown is still at least six months in the future. Only then will officials determine which areas are safe enough for evacuees to return. They will measure the dangerous radioactive isotopes in the soil and water. Some places will only be safe after the top layer of soil has been carted away. Others might not be safe for years.

COMPARING FUKUSHIMA TO TMI AND CHERNOBYL

Almost as soon as the news comes of the Fukushima meltdowns, official investigations begin. They all ask the same question: was Fukushima more like TMI or Chernobyl?

To answer that, scientists will study the meltdowns and the spread of radioactivity at Fukushima Daiichi for years to come. But we already know enough about the disaster to say that it is much worse than TMI and not as bad as Chernobyl.

TMI had only a single meltdown and only a minor release of radioactivity. Fukushima had three meltdowns plus problems in the spent fuel storage pools. It had two large explosions and several fires.

TMI had no measurable health effects, not even among the power plant workers. It led to only a short evacuation of pregnant women and children over a small distance. Fukushima has forced tens of thousands

A woman in Ishinomaki, Japan, stares in shock at the damage caused by the tsunami. The emotional toll among people impacted by the natural and nuclear disasters includes sleeplessness, anxiety, and depression.

of people out of their homes for months. It has exposed them to a small amount of extra radiation.

The workers bringing the Fukushima Daiichi to cold shutdown will face some health concerns later in life. A few have had mishaps that exposed them to serious levels of radioactivity. The rest have been adding to their total radiation dose with every hour of work. That gives them a higher than average cancer risk though not a certainty of the disease.

The total health impact of Fukushima's radiation is much less than Chernobyl's. The Chernobyl meltdown began with a raging, smoky fire that turned an entire reactor core into dust. The firefighters who battled it faced deadly levels of radiation.

Smoke from Chernobyl's burning graphite core released seven times as much radiation as the Fukushima meltdowns. Contamination from Chernobyl spread far from the power plant. The radiation from Fukushima caused very little threat beyond the evacuation zone.

Still, Fukushima's impact on human lives is huge. How do you measure what it means to be forced out of your home or off your farmland?

Beyond the damage and human costs, Fukushima also raises serious questions about nuclear power plants in the future. Will nuclear power bounce back just as it did after TMI and Chernobyl? Or has the industry suffered a meltdown from which it will never recover?

Chapter 5

FUKUSHIMA
AND OUR
ENERGY FUTURE

We live in a world of technology that is powered by electricity. To generate that electricity, we need a source of energy. That energy can come from many sources. We can burn coal, oil, or other fuels. We can use the energy of fast-flowing water. We can use energy from the wind. We can capture energy from sunlight. Or we can use nuclear energy.

As long as there has been nuclear power, some people have argued that it is too dangerous under any circumstances. Ever since the Fukushima disaster, those arguments have been louder and more frequent.

Four days after the Great Tohoku Earthquake, the *Japan Times* ran an editorial that criticized both the government and the power companies. "The events that have unfolded at the nuclear power plants in Fukushima make it clear that the government and the power industry have failed to implement necessary safeguards," it noted.

The day before that, Tokyo's Citizen's Nuclear Information Center held a press conference for foreign journalists. One of the speakers was Masashi Goto, who once worked as a nuclear power plant designer. He said that government and power plant companies didn't design their reactors to survive major quakes. That includes the company he worked for—the one that designed four of the six Fukushima Daiichi reactors.

"I have been worrying about nuclear power plants since the Kashi-wazaki-Kariwa nuclear power plant was damaged," he said, speaking about a 2007 quake that measured 6.8 on the Richter scale. "If the authorities decide to build more nuclear power plants, they should set criteria based on a thorough examination of any possible natural disasters."

HOW SAFE ARE NUCLEAR POWER PLANTS?

Not everyone agrees that nuclear power has to be dangerous. Many people in many countries see a place for nuclear technology in their energy future. If we pay attention to the risks, they say, nuclear power plants can be much better for the world than fossil fuel (mainly coal- and oil-burning) plants.

One major problem with fossil fuel plants is air pollution. Devices called scrubbers remove most of the dangerous pollutants from the exhaust of fossil fuel plants. Everyone agrees those pollutants can be harmful. But that doesn't stop people from arguing about how strict government regulations on those substances should be.

In recent years, another very significant concern about fossil fuels has arisen. Adding too much carbon dioxide (CO_2) to the air can change the world's climate in serious ways. Burning fossil fuels produces lots of CO_2. Nuclear power produces none. So scientists and political leaders ask these questions: Can we replace nuclear power plants and still have

Coal is a major source of electrical energy in the United States and around the world. This coal train is miles long.

all the electricity we need? Can we replace nuclear power plants and still protect Earth's climate?

Engineers know that people make mistakes. They know that materials and structures can fail, especially as they get older. They know what kinds of hazards can cause problems—including severe weather, earthquakes and tsunamis, and terrorist attacks.

They also know how to build power plants that will survive all of those events. At worst, even if the plants are destroyed, safety precautions can ensure that people and property will survive unharmed. But if engineers already know how to build safe nuclear power plants, what can we say about TMI, Chernobyl, and Fukushima?

Nuclear power plant technology can be safe. Yet TMI had a meltdown because its operators didn't recognize a problem. And an important notice that could have helped those operators didn't reach them in time. Even so, the damage from the TMI meltdown was limited to the plant itself.

Nuclear power plant technology can be safe. Yet the explosion at Chernobyl happened because its operators did not realize how serious a risk they were taking in testing the plant's safety system. In addition, they did not have rules that could have prevented them from doing the test in the first place. Their actions led to thousands of cases of cancer over a large area. The city of Pripyat and the region surrounding Chernobyl had to be abandoned.

Investigators inspect Fukushima's reactor 3 three months after the meltdown at the plant. Cleanup efforts are slow and are sometimes slowed further by unanticipated problems related to safely disposing of contaminated water at the site. As a result, many people around the world are asking difficult questions about the value of nuclear power, given its potential dangers.

Nuclear power plant technology can be safe. Yet the Fukushima Daiichi power plant suffered three meltdowns, two major explosions, and several fires that sent radioactivity into the environment. None of those failures should have happened.

The reactors at Fukushima Daiichi were designed to withstand the worst earthquake and tsunami that had ever happened in that area before. But it did not survive the Great Tohoku Earthquake—even though scientists knew a quake that powerful was bound to happen eventually.

Scientists have only been able to measure earthquakes accurately for a little more than one hundred years. The Tohoku quake is the most powerful to hit Japan since then. But it is only the fifth most powerful earthquake on record, and the four stronger ones have all happened since 1952.

The 9.0 earthquake certainly falls within the realm of "any possible natural disasters," the recommended basis for safety criteria from Masashi Goto. Fukushima Daiichi reactor 1 should have withstood it, but it didn't.

Engineers knew that boiling water reactors like the ones at Fukushima had design flaws. Those could lead to meltdowns in a large earthquake and tsunami. They also knew that newer reactor designs would come through a Tohoku-like event without serious damage.

They had already begun planning for replacement reactors at Fukushima. But TEPCO wanted to stretch out the life of reactor 1, and government regulators allowed them to take that risk.

CLIMATE CHANGE AND NUCLEAR POWER

Why would any government take the risk of using nuclear power? Because the world is heading for a crisis caused mainly by burning too much coal and oil. Burning those fossil fuels produces CO_2.

Carbon dioxide is different from other gases and soot that pollute the air. Life on Earth depends on CO_2, even though it is just a small part of our atmosphere. It helps trap heat to keep Earth warm enough for life. But too much of it can make Earth's climate too warm.

We are probably already seeing the early effects of that extra energy in the atmosphere. Heat waves, droughts, and dangerous storms have become more common. Signs of spring are coming earlier and fall is lingering longer. Plants and animals are moving farther from the equator or to higher altitudes to find the moderate climates they need. Tropical diseases are spreading.

A stream of water flows off the huge ice sheet that covers Greenland. Most scientists agree that the ice sheet is melting faster because of global warming.

Scientists are continually evaluating new data to determine if these changes are permanent and directly due to the extra CO_2. But this much is already certain. The changes match experts' predictions of what a warmer world will be like.

Even the polar ice sheets—the huge glaciers covering Antarctica and Greenland—are showing signs of melting. Making exact predictions is hard, but warmer oceans and melting icecaps could raise sea levels by 2 m (6 ft) by 2100.

In future centuries, the problem could be much worse. Many low-lying coastal areas would be flooded. Cities would be destroyed or transformed. Millions of residents of low-lying areas, such as large portions of the nation of Bangladesh, might be forced to move to another country entirely.

The world can head off the worst problems of climate change by using forms of energy that do not add CO_2 to the air. Nuclear energy has been one of the solutions over the past few decades. But the disaster at Fukushima has forced the world to reconsider the benefits versus the dangers.

IS NUCLEAR POWER WORTH THE RISK?

It will be many years before we know the full impact of Fukushima. How many people will die or get cancer from radioactivity? How much farmland will be lost for how long? How much seafood will be contaminated? How bad will the damage to the Japanese and world economies be?

In the months immediately following Fukushima, those questions echoed around the world. Every nuclear power plant was examined for risks. Almost every national government took a fresh look at its regulations. The leaders of every industrialized country looked at their future energy needs. Even in developing countries that included nuclear power as part of their future, the same big question arose: should they change their energy plans?

Should they shut down nuclear power plants sooner than planned? Or should they replace those power plants with updated nuclear technology? Should they not replace them at all and use less electricity? Or should they replace them with other, less risky sources of energy?

Different countries answered those questions in different ways. After the Japanese disaster, Germany quickly disconnected eight of its seventeen nuclear power plants, announcing it would close the remaining nine by 2022. The German government announced plans to use more solar and wind power in the future.

Even France, where about 75 percent of its electricity comes from nuclear power, plans to take a second look at its energy options. "No scenario will be left out, including the scenario of exiting nuclear power," says energy minister Eric Besson. But he thinks France is not likely to drop nuclear's share below two-thirds of the nation's total electricity use.

China, the country growing fastest in demand for electricity, announced that it may build fewer new nuclear power plants than planned. But it will still satisfy much of its growing need for electricity with large numbers of them.

France gets almost all of its electricity from nuclear power. After the disaster in Japan, French antinuclear protesters gathered in Paris in June 2011. The sign says: "It's possible! Denmark, Austria, and Germany have ditched nuclear power. Why not France?"

India's need for power is also growing fast. The country has large nuclear fuel resources and the advanced technology to build power reactors. So the Indian government has set a goal of producing 25 percent of its electricity from nuclear plants by 2050. The Indian government has promised stronger safety regulations, but some Indian people remain strongly against nuclear power. In the western state of Maharashta, demonstrations against a planned nuclear power station in April 2011 turned violent.

In the United States, most companies are taking a wait-and-see approach. That follows the pattern after TMI and Chernobyl. After TMI, many U.S. power companies canceled orders for new nuclear reactors. Interest in nuclear power finally began to come back in 2001. But it wasn't until 2010 that any power company broke ground for a new nuclear plant.

Fukushima will certainly make it harder to get a U.S. license for a new nuclear power plant in the next few years. But it is too soon to say whether the Japanese disaster will have a major impact on electric power in the United States in the long run.

"GREEN" ALTERNATIVES TO NUCLEAR POWER

The nuclear power industry made a strong recovery after TMI and Chernobyl. Will it do the same after Fukushima? The answer to that question depends on other technologies for producing electricity that do not add CO_2 to the air. These are often called renewable, sustainable, or "green" technologies.

Let's look at the most promising green technologies for the world's energy future.

HYDROELECTRICITY, OR HYDROELECTRIC POWER. Using flowing water to drive electric generators has been an important source of electricity for a long time. In the United States, about 6 percent of the electricity comes from hydroelectric plants.

It is easy to see how much energy is available at a place like Niagara Falls (which straddles the border between New York and Ontario). A hydroelectric plant there provided small amounts of electricity as early as the 1860s. Since early in the twentieth century, both the United States and Canada have had major power plants on opposite shores of the Niagara River.

Hydroelectric dams, such as this one in Montana, provide a much safer form of energy than do nuclear power plants. However, building dams often requires the flooding of towns, relocating citizens, and the flooding of historical or geographical treasures.

Producing hydroelectricity is not as simple as placing a generator in a fast-flowing stream. The water needs to be controlled, which means building a dam. The more electricity the power plants produce, the more water they send over the dams. So the flow over the famous falls is reduced.

Hydroelectric power plants can create environmental problems. In the United States Pacific Northwest, power companies have had to build fish ladders around dams so salmon can get upstream to their breeding places. The dams and ladders interfere with some Native American tribes' traditional salmon fishing grounds.

In Egypt the Aswan High Dam, completed in 1970s, blocked the Nile River's natural flow of silt (particles of soil and rock) and changed the pattern of annual floods. Without that silt and flooding, the Nile Valley is not as naturally fertile as it used to be. The change in flow also increased the number of snails in that area that cause a disease in humans called schistosomiasis.

China's Three Gorges Dam, completed in 2006, may be the most harmful hydroelectric project in history. At first, the Chinese government denied the problems. But in 2008, they admitted that "the massive hydroelectric dam, sandwiched between breathtaking cliffs on the Yangtze River in central China, may be triggering landslides, altering entire ecosystems and causing other serious environmental problems."

So should the world stop using hydroelectricity? No, not as long as people balance their needs with environmental concerns. But even though hydroelectric power is renewable, the number of places where it can be produced is limited. It will probably remain an important but small source of electricity in our energy future.

GEOTHERMAL ENERGY. The heat inside Earth is another sustainable source of electricity. If it is hot enough to melt the mantle rocks, it is certainly hot enough to boil water to run an electric generator.

In most places on Earth, you would have to dig miles beneath the crust to reach that heat. But in a few places, it comes close to the surface or even bursts through. In the United States, the most famous site for geothermal energy is Yellowstone Park. But other areas have geysers, hot springs, and even volcanoes.

Using geothermal energy doesn't cause any notable harm to the environment. But there are not very many places where it is practical. The United States leads the world in geothermal electricity production. But the total amount of geothermal electricity produced is about as much as three or four nuclear reactors—or ten average-sized coal-fired power plants—provide.

The United States has about one hundred nuclear reactors and six hundred coal-fired power plants producing electricity. That means geothermal can only play a small part in replacing coal or nuclear power.

WIND POWER. Huge wind turbines are springing up all around the world from Denmark to Denver, Colorado, to Djibouti. Power companies usually place several turbines close together. Often so many turbines cover a large area that people call it a wind farm.

Wind turbines produce affordable, renewable energy. But they have a few disadvantages. Their spinning blades are hazardous for birds and bats. Some people oppose them for the harm they cause to animals. Others note that bats eat insects and some birds eat rodents. With fewer bats and birds, more of those pests survive to cause problems for nearby farmers.

Many people living in scenic coastal regions also object to wind farms. They often fight power companies because turbines disrupt the view, which hurts property value.

The biggest disadvantage of a wind farm is the amount of open space it needs. The world's largest wind farm, the Horse Hollow Wind Energy Center in Texas, covers 47,000 acres (19,000 hectares). That's more than twice the area of New York's Manhattan Island. It has 421 turbines

and produces enough energy to power 220,000 homes. That sounds like a lot, but it is less than one-third of the power produced by an average nuclear reactor—or about one-twentieth of what the six Fukushima Daiichi reactors produced before the Tohoku earthquake.

Still, wind power is growing fast. Even if it doesn't replace nuclear power, it will be an important energy source for replacing fossil fuels in the years ahead.

SOLAR POWER. After Fukushima, Germany announced plans to replace all of its nuclear power plants with renewable energy by 2022. Wind power is part of its strategy. But using solar power (turning sunlight into electricity) is an even bigger part.

Germany has been one of the world's leading nations in using solar power. That is surprising given its location in northern Europe. Sunlight is much less direct there than in areas closer to Earth's equator. But the Germans have shown that there is plenty of useful sunlight almost anywhere people call home.

Germany's solar electricity power comes from photovoltaic (PV) cells, which convert the energy of sunlight directly into electricity. Large panels of PV cells have powered spacecraft for many years. More recently, they have become affordable enough for power plants on Earth.

Solar energy is more concentrated than wind power. But a solar power plant still needs a lot more space than a fossil-fuel or nuclear power

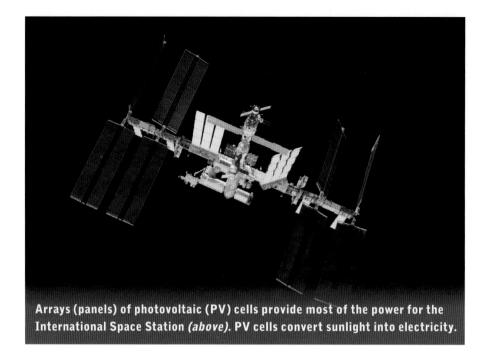

Arrays (panels) of photovoltaic (PV) cells provide most of the power for the International Space Station *(above)*. PV cells convert sunlight into electricity.

plant. Germany has been producing most of its solar electricity from large installations like the Waldpolenz Solar Park.

Waldpolenz is the world's largest PV power station. It was completed in 2008 and covers about 220 ha (550 ac). That's about as large as seven hundred American football fields, including the end zones. Yet it only produces one-fortieth of the power of a single nuclear reactor.

In the future, much of Germany's solar power will come from PV panels on roofs of homes and buildings. That will make it easier to find space to generate solar electricity.

Home solar panels are expensive. The German plan includes a way for residents to afford them. On sunny days, rooftop solar panels produce more electricity than most households need. When that happens, the customers sell electricity to the power company instead of the other way around!

THE POLITICS OF ELECTRIC POWER

So what will our energy future look like? Will we reduce fossil fuel burning and avoid major climate problems?

Answering those questions leads us to questions about the technology of generating electricity. Only the future will tell us if nuclear power can recover from Fukushima. Part of the answer depends on whether wind, solar, hydroelectric, and geothermal can produce enough electricity at a low enough cost.

But more important than the technological questions are political ones. Both governments and citizens will be faced with difficult choices.

Before the Fukushima meltdowns, twenty-five years had passed since the last major nuclear accident at Chernobyl. Although the public debate over nuclear energy quieted down, the arguments remained the same.

Now those arguments are louder than ever. Both sides agree that TMI, Chernobyl, and Fukushima have important lessons to teach. But they disagree about what those lessons are.

The antinuclear side says that the lessons teach us that nuclear power plant technology will always be too risky to try. The pronuclear side says that we have learned the lessons of failure. They argue that we know how to make nuclear power plants much safer and that we can succeed in spite of the risks.

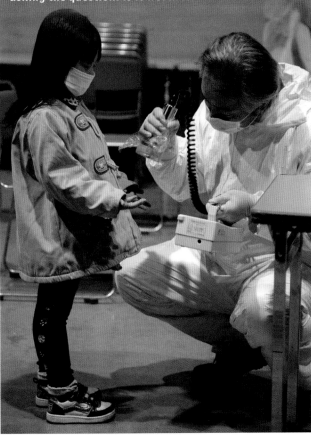

An official checks a little girl in Koriyama, Fukushima Prefecture, for radiation. Nuclear disasters put the future of young people at risk. Ever since the Fukushima nuclear disaster, many global citizens are asking the question: is it worth it?

They also argue that climate change poses a much greater risk to the whole world than another meltdown. We can't afford to stop building nuclear power plants, they say, if it means burning more coal or oil.

THE DECISION IS YOURS

In 2036, when Fukushima is as far in the past as Chernobyl was in 2011, the world's use of electricity will be very different. And so will the laws and regulations about nuclear power.

By then you may be an engineer whose work

Clean Coal?

Coal is the most plentiful source of energy to produce electric power. It is also the least expensive. So many electric power companies are looking for ways to use it while releasing less CO_2 into the air.

They already use scrubbers to remove many pollutants before they come out of the smokestacks. That makes coal cleaner, but it doesn't solve the problem of climate change. So some companies, like American Electric Power (AEP), have been working on projects to capture CO_2 in the smokestacks and bury it underground.

They call it clean coal. Beginning in 2009, AEP successfully tested a small clean coal project in West Virginia. They planned to build a much larger one but changed their minds in 2011. Clean coal power costs more, and AEP did not think the state would allow the company to charge more for electricity.

The company had also expected the U.S. Congress to pass a law limiting CO_2 or charging for putting out too much. That never happened, so they put the project on hold.

"This is what happens when you don't get a climate bill," a U.S. government official told the *New York Times*. One of the most promising technologies to reduce CO_2 has been set back many years.

creates better electric power plants. Or you may be a political leader who helps make laws and regulations. But no matter what you choose to do with your life and no matter where in the world you live, you will have an opportunity to vote.

Your vote will provide guidance to those political leaders. Your vote will influence what the regulations should be about nuclear power.

It will be up to you to make sure we have strong laws to protect the environment and to limit climate change caused by humans. It will be up to you to make sure we have regulations that require safe design of nuclear power plants.

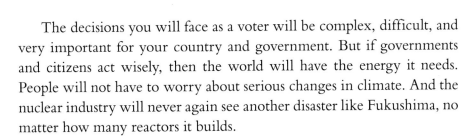

As in Japan, nuclear power plants in the United States are vulnerable to natural disasters. For example, floodwaters surrounded the Fort Calhoun nuclear power plant in Nebraska in June 2011. The plant remained safe, but some people became fearful of a malfunction because of the recent Fukushima meltdowns. Young people can be part of the future by helping to make sure that all our sources of energy are safe and healthy.

The decisions you will face as a voter will be complex, difficult, and very important for your country and government. But if governments and citizens act wisely, then the world will have the energy it needs. People will not have to worry about serious changes in climate. And the nuclear industry will never again see another disaster like Fukushima, no matter how many reactors it builds.

And the credit for that happy future will belong to people like you.

GLOSSARY

alpha radiation: a form of radioactivity in which the nucleus sends out a helium nucleus with high energy

beta radiation: a form of radioactivity in which the nucleus sends out an electron with high energy

chain reaction: a process in which fission neutrons set off fissions in other nuclei until most of the fissionable nuclei have undergone fission

cold shutdown: a condition in which a reactor core no longer needs a flow of cooling water to keep it from melting

control rod: a rod that absorbs neutrons and can move into and out of a reactor's core

cooling water: water that absorbs heat from a nuclear reactor and carries it to where its energy can create the steam that drives an electrical generator

critical mass: the amount of mass necessary to cause a chain reaction in a fissionable material

crust: Earth's rocky outer layer

earthquake: a sudden, powerful shifting of part of Earth's rocky outer layer or crust

electron: a small, light particle in an atom that carries a negative electric charge

epicenter: the place on Earth's surface directly above the underground spot where an earthquake begins

fission: a radioactive process in which a nucleus breaks up into two smaller nuclei and several neutrons that carry high energy

focus: the place under Earth where moving plates slip to start an earthquake, also called the hypocenter

fuel rod: a cylinder, which is made of an alloy that does not corrode and which does not absorb many neutrons, that contains pellets of fissionable material

gamma radiation: a form of radioactivity in which the nucleus sends a burst of energy like a powerful X-ray

half-life: the time it takes for half of the nuclei of a radioactive material to disintegrate

hydroelectricity: electricity produced by using rapidly flowing water to drive a generator, also called hydroelectric power

isotope: one of several forms of a nucleus of an element with the same number of protons and a different number of neutrons

meltdown: a kind of accident in a nuclear reactor in which the fuel rods melt

moderator: a substance that slows down fission neutrons so they have a better chance of causing another fission

neutron: a neutrally charged particle in an atom's nucleus

nucleon: a proton or a neutron

nucleus (plural nuclei): the small central part of an atom that contains most of its mass

plate: a section of Earth's rocky outer layer (or crust)

prefecture: a Japanese state or province

protron: a particle in an atom's nucleus that carries a positive electric charge

P-wave: a vibration from an earthquake that is a sound wave with a pitch much too low to be heard. It may be felt, but it causes little damage. It is called a primary wave because it travels faster and arrives before the S-wave, or secondary wave.

radioactivity: a phenomenon in which the nucleus of an atom sends out a burst of energy

reactor core: the portion of a nuclear reactor where it generates its energy

renewable energy: a form of energy that flows naturally and that we can use but not use up

Richter scale: the most common scale used to measure the strength of an earthquake

S-wave: a powerful, often damaging earthquake vibration that shakes the ground up and down or back and forth. It is called a secondary wave because it travels more slowly than the P-wave, or primary wave, and thus arrives later.

spent fuel: reactor fuel that is no longer useful for producing a chain reaction

Tohoku: the region of Japan at the northern end of the main island of Honshu. It consists of six prefectures.

tsunami: a Japanese word for "harbor wave," a powerful destructive wall of water that rushes in from the sea

turbine: a device that spins to generate power, such as the steam-driven turbines in nuclear power plants or wind-driven turbines in wind farms

SOURCE NOTES

4   Arun Vemuri, "Cakes," in *2:46: Aftershocks: Stories from the Japan Earthquake*, ed. Patrick Sherriff (London: Enhanced Editions Ltd., 2011), Kindle Edition.

4   Ibid.

5   Eric Talmadge, and Mari Yamaguchi, "How First 24 Hours Shaped Japan's Nuclear Crisis," Associated Press, July 3, 2011, available online at http://news.yahoo.com/first-24-hours-shaped-japans-nuclear-crisis-060035933.html (October 17, 2011).

28 Mike Gray, and Ira Rosen, *The Warning: Accident at Three Mile Island* (Chicago: Contemporary Books, 1982), 27.

31 Fred Bortz, *Catastrophe! Great Engineering Failure—and Success* (New York: W. H. Freeman, 1995), 55.

33 Richard L. Thornbaugh, quoted in *Pittsburgh Tribune-Review* interview, available online at "Audio: Dick Thornburgh on TMI Accident," March 22, 2009, http://www.pittsburghlive.com/x/pittsburghtrib/news/multimedia/s_617234.html (October 17, 2011).

34 Jake Adelstein, and David McNeill, "Meltdown: What Really Happened at Fukushima?" *Atlantic Wire*, July 2, 2011, http://www.theatlanticwire.com/global/2011/07/meltdown-what-really-happened-fukushima/39541/ (October 19, 2011).

53 Ibid.

35 Talmadge and Yamaguchi, "How First 24 Hours Shaped Japan's Nuclear Crisis."

36 Ibid.

42 *Japan Times*, "Editorial: Nuclear Power in Disarray," March 15, 2011. http://www.japantimes.co.jp/text/ed20110315a1.html (October 19, 2011).

43 Eriko Arita, "Disaster Analysis You May Not Hear Elsewhere," *Japan Times*, March 20, 2011. http://www.japantimes.co.jp/text/fl20110320x2.html (October 19, 2011).

47 Robin Sayles, "France Includes Nuclear Exit Scenario in Study on Energy Policy," Platts, July 11, 2011, http://www.platts.com/RSSFeedDetailedNews/RSSFeed/ElectricPower/6262761 (October 17, 2011).

49 Mara Hvistendahl, "China's Three Gorges Dam: An Environmental Catastrophe?" *Scientific American*, March 25, 2008, http://www.scientificamerican.com/article.cfm?id=chinas-three-gorges-dam-disaster (October 17, 2011).

54 Matthew L. Wald and John M. Broder, "Utility Shelves Ambitious Plan to Limit Carbon," *New York Times*, July 13, 2011, http://www.nytimes.com/2011/07/14/business/energy-environment/utility-shelves-plan-to-capture-carbon-dioxide.html (October 17, 2011).

SELECTED BIBLIOGRAPHY

Adelstein, Jake, and David McNeill, "Meltdown: What Really Happened at Fukushima?" *Atlantic Wire*, July 2, 2011. http://www.theatlanticwire.com/global/2011/07/meltdown-what-really-happened-fukushima/39541/ (October 19, 2011).

Birmingham, Lucy, "Japan's Earthquake Warning System Explained. *Time*, March 18, 2011. http://www.time.com/time/world/article/0,8599,2059780,00.html (October 17, 2011).

Gray, Mike, and Ira Rosen. *The Warning: Accident at Three Mile Island*. 1982. Reprint, New York: W. W. Norton, 2003.

Knight, Will, "How Japan's Earthquake and Tsunami Warning Systems Work." *Technology Review*, March 11, 2011. http://www.technologyreview.com/blog/editors/26505/ (October 17, 2011).

Sherriff, Patrick, ed. *2:46 Aftershocks: Stories from the Japan Earthquake*. London: Enhanced Editions, 2011.

Talmadge, Eric, and Mari Yamaguchi, "How First 24 Hours Shaped Japan's Nuclear Crisis." Associated Press, July 3, 2011. Available online at http://news.yahoo.com/first-24-hours-shaped-japans-nuclear-crisis-060035933.html (October 17, 2011).

FURTHER READING

Bortz, Fred. *Catastrophe! Great Engineering Failure—and Success*. New York: W. H. Freeman, 1995 (Especially Chapter 5, "Fission With Melted Roads," about Three Mile Island and Chernobyl).

————. *The Neutron*. New York: Rosen, 2004.

————. *Physics: Decade by Decade* (Twentieth-Century Science). New York: Facts on File, 2007 (Especially Chapter 4, 1931-1940: Particles and Politics and Chapter 5, 1941-1950: Physics in a Time of War).

————. *Seven Wonders of Exploration Technology*. Minneapolis: Twenty-First Century Books, 2010.

Hamilton, Janet. *Lise Meitner: Pioneer of Nuclear Fission*. Great Minds of Science series. Springfield, NJ: PUBLISHER TK1997.

Johnson, Rebecca L. *Atomic Structure*. Minneapolis: Twenty-First Century Books, 2008.

————. *Plate Tectonics*. Minneapolis: Twenty-First Century Books, 2006.

Morris, Ann. *Tsunami: Helping Each Other*. Minneapolis: Millbrook Press, 2006.

Pringle, Laurence. *Living in a Risky World*. New York: William Morrow & Co., 1989. (Written not long after Chernobyl, this book and the next one by Laurence Pringle are still extremely valuable for understanding the public mood at that time. The questions that arose then are still important in the twenty-first century.)

————. *Nuclear Energy: Troubled Past, Uncertain Future*. New York: Macmillan, 1989.

Silverstein, Alvin, Virginia Silverstein, and Laura Silverstein Nunn. *Global Warming*. Minneapolis: Twenty-First Century Books, 2009.

WEBSITES

International Atomic Energy Agency
http://www.iaea.org/
https://www.facebook.com/iaeaorg
The IAEA is an agency of the United Nations that gathers information about nuclear weapons and nuclear power. Immediately after the Fukushima meltdowns, it established a Web page with reports and updates at http://www.iaea.org/newscenter/news/tsunamiupdate01.html.

The Japan Times webpage for Tohoku earthquake news
http://www.japantimes.co.jp/news/tohoku-kanto-earthquake-news.html
The *Japan Times* is an English language newspaper with balanced news coverage and a variety of opinions in its editorials and letters to the editor.

Meltdown! — "Dr. Fred's Place"
http://www.fredbortz.com/Meltdown
The author's Web pages for this book includes links for news and updates from Fukushima.

New York Times Website Special Section, "Japan — Earthquake, Tsunami and Nuclear Crisis (2011)"
(http://topics.nytimes.com/top/news/international/countriesandterritories/japan/index.html?scp=1)
The *New York Times* is generally regarded as one of the leading newspapers of record in the United States. Its website includes special sections like this one that collect articles on major topics and are particularly valuable for researching a major event like the Fukushima disaster.

LERNER
SOURCE

Expand learning beyond the printed book. Download free, complementary educational resources for this book from our website, www.lerneresource.com.

INDEX

AUTHOR'S NOTE

I wrote this book in the spring and summer of 2011, only months after the Great Tohoku Earthquake and tsunami, and I continued updating it with new information until it went to press. That means I had to rely on newspapers and magazines, mostly online, for information. I subscribe to *New Scientist* and *Science News* magazines. Both of those are known for excellent journalism that goes into greater science and engineering detail than most daily newspapers. They were valuable sources for understanding what happened during the earthquake and tsunami and what was happening at Fukushima.

I especially wanted information directly from Japan, but I do not speak Japanese. So I was delighted to discover the English-language *Japan Times* website (http://www.japantimes.co.jp/). I scanned its daily headlines from March 12, 2011, forward. I read every article about the event and paid special attention to the news from Fukushima. Its news coverage was balanced, its editorials were thoughtful, and its letters from readers reflected a variety of viewpoints.

One of the *Japan Times* articles led me to a collection of personal experiences during the earthquake in an e-book called *2:46 Aftershocks: Stories from the Japan Earthquake* written by the Quakebook Community. It is now also available as a paperback.

I get a daily e-mail with links to science news stories from Sigma Xi, the Scientific Research Society, plus occasional pointers to news articles from friends who know what I am writing. Many useful links arrived just in time to help me shape my thoughts.

Finally, the Wikipedia online encyclopedia is a useful place to look for information on developing news stories, but it is not completely trustworthy. I never used its information directly, but its footnotes and links helped me find sources that I could verify.

Just as I did not rely on only one source in writing this book, readers should go beyond this book to understand the events of the Great Tohoku Earthquake and tsunami and the meltdowns at Fukushima Daiichi. And since news is always changing, I have created a page on my website (www.fredbortz.com/Meltdown) where you can find the latest information, including links to news and information sites.

—*Fred Bortz, Monroeville, PA, October 2011*

ABOUT THE AUTHOR

After earning his PhD at Carnegie Mellon University in 1971, physicist Fred Bortz set off on an interesting and varied twenty-five-year career in teaching and research. From 1974 to 1977, he was a senior engineer at Westinghouse Advanced Reactors Division, where he applied his skills in computer modeling to reactor core design. In 1979 he returned to Carnegie Mellon, where his work evolved from research to outreach over a fifteen-year period, during which he also began publishing books about science and technology for young readers.

Dr. Bortz published his third book, *Catastrophe! Great Engineering Failure—and Success*, in 1995. When it was designated a "Selector's Choice" on the 1996 list of Outstanding Science Trade Books for Children, he decided to spend the rest of his career as a full-time writer. *Catastrophe*'s most notable chapter, "Fission with Melted Rods," discussed the lessons of the nuclear meltdowns at Three Mile Island and Chernobyl. Rather than giving readers answers, it left them with questions that they would face as adults.

Meltdown!—his twentieth book—picks up where that chapter left off. The questions remain the same, but the world is very different. Does nuclear energy have a future after the triple meltdown at the Fukushima Daiichi power plant? Does the rise of wind and solar power mean we can avoid nuclear power? Or does global warming mean we need it more than ever? These are vital questions for citizens of the future. *Meltdown!* can help them explore the answers.

PHOTO ACKNOWLEDGMENTS